The P
Fátima, Garabandal, Akita and Bayside

Dates of the Garabandal Warning,
Garabandal Miracle and
End of the World Revealed

Sean Murphy

Acknowledgments

I want to begin by thanking Robert Franzenburg for sharing the miraculous Jacinta 1972 photo with the world.

Lorenzo Franciosi and Steve Alexander, thank you for granting me permission to use your images.

John Paul Wohlscheid at tldm.org, thanks for your help.

Thanks to Lucia Santos, Francisco Marto and Jacinta Marto of Fátima, Portugal. Thanks to Conchita Gonzalez, Jacinta Gonzalez, Mari Loli Mazon and Mari Cruz Gonzalez of Garabandal, Spain. Thanks to Agnes Sasagawa of Akita, Japan. Thanks to Veronica Lueken of Bayside, New York. And thanks to all others who have selflessly contributed to this incredible story and kept the light of God burning in this tired and worn world. You all have my deepest gratitude.

Thank you to Our Heavenly Father. It has been the greatest privilege and honour of my life to reveal the truth in this work.

Contents

List of Figures

Preface

I am forty-seven years old from County Derry in the north of Ireland. I was raised a Catholic and always had a desire within to try to establish God's fundamental truths that govern this world. I was somewhat adept at religious education at secondary school, but it wasn't until several years later when I turned nineteen that I had what I would describe as my first encounter with God.

While going through a very traumatic time in my life, I had an experience where I felt the presence of God in both mind and body. The interaction which was in essence an awakening of my consciousness to something greater than myself gave me the strength to carry on. What happened that day has remained with me through the entire course of my life.

Having completed my BEng and MSc at Queen's University in Belfast, I had a very close brush with death. This led to further suffering which would act as the catalyst for what was to follow. My life had become very solitary. This was at a time when 56k modem dial up was the standard for accessing the internet and I would leave my computer running in the hallway of our home when downloading files. The computer would go into sleep mode but many times as I approached from a distance, it would awaken without my touch. I couldn't understand what was happening at the time, but looking back, I feel a presence was with me.

I kept a Bible next to my bedside with the intention of studying the texts to try to uncover the grand scheme of life but my spiritual journey, or beginning of awakening the mind to remembrance of God, began in 2004 with a simple prayer. I could also feel a presence trying to pull me away from the journey I was about to embark on. I could never have imagined what was going to unfold in the coming years.

In the summer of 2006, on a day with brilliant clear blue skies, just after sunset, I saw the sun's binary twin and its orbitals. I knew with certainty from that point in time that the end of this age was drawing near. In the summer of 2007, I had my second encounter with God. Alone in a room, a spirit appeared resembling an orb of light that remained with me for several minutes before slowly fading away. This second encounter was an affirmation of the visible as opposed to the thought or feeling of the first encounter. No word was spoken but again it was a reassurance of life existing beyond this current space and time continuum or world that we live in.

Several years passed with small incremental changes in awareness. In 2016, during silent meditation, I felt the joy of God for the first time; a feeling emanating from the heart extending into the mind that cannot be explained through the use of words. It was an ecstatic feeling so far beyond anything I had ever experienced in this material world.

I have always believed that the date of the end of this age could be known. In 2019, while browsing the internet using a second hand iPhone 4S that my mother had bought me as a Christmas present, I came across the Jacinta 1972 photograph. It captured my imagination and I knew that it contained an unspoken truth. As a qualified mechanical engineer with an analytical mind geared towards problem solving with over fifteen years of extensive research in spiritual matters, perhaps I may be capable of unlocking the puzzle containing the most important information in the world.

Introduction

I t took two years to find the solution to the Jacinta 1972 photograph. The purpose of this book is to provide the reader with enough knowledge to see the logical steps taken to solve the puzzle. It is my hope that the dates of the Garabandal warning, Garabandal miracle and end of the world revealed in this photo will be seen as certain as opposed to mere speculation.

This will be a short discourse focusing primarily on numerology, presenting the data that fits into the puzzle revealing the solutions. This photo is one of the greatest gift's God has ever given to humanity. Those that are blessed to discover this information will not be caught unaware as these events begin to unfold in the near future. They will be forearmed with the knowledge that provides a foundation to take decisive action to help themselves and those that they love.

This is a compelling story spanning over a hundred years containing many miracles. It is a message of hope for all those that are suffering or have, are or will go through unbearable pain. Even when things seem to be at their worst, the Garabandal miracle will give us the strength to continue towards this great day of destiny. The date of the last day of this world revealed in this book is graduation day. This is an incredible time to be alive.

Procuring the Data Related to the Puzzle

The Miracle of the Sun at Fátima

The miracle of the sun at Fátima was a simulation portending events that would occur in Earth's future. The sudden dropping of the sun towards Earth was related to the coming warning of Garabandal in which Earth will be struck by two asteroids. The sun changing colours and appearing to shine with each colour of the rainbow, which lasted for approximately 10 minutes, was related to the colours that will appear at the Garabandal miracle; an event also lasting just over ten minutes.

The apparent dancing of the sun in the sky was a simulation of a violently wobbling Earth in the month of October in a given year in Earth's future leading into the last weeks of this age. An event that would fulfil the prophecy of Isaiah 24:20, "The earth is utterly broken apart, the earth is split open, the earth is shaken violently.

The earth staggers like a drunkard and sways like a shack. Earth's rebellion ways it down, and it falls, never to rise again. In that day the LORD will punish the host of heaven above and the kings of the earth below...”[1]

The apparitions of Our Lady of Fátima witnessed by Lucia Santos, Jacinta and Francisco Marto took place on the thirteenth day of each month from May to October 1917, excluding August when the children could not arrive on the thirteenth of that month.[2] Fátima is clearly number 13.

The Garabandal Warning, Miracle and Date of the End

The apparitions of Our Lady of Garabandal witnessed by Conchita Gonzalez, Jacinta Gonzalez, Mari Loli Mazon and Mari Cruz Gonzalez took place between 1961 and 1965.[3] The most well-known apparitions and events took place on June 18th 1961, July 2nd 1961, August 8th 1961, October 18th 1961, July 18th 1962, June 18th 1965 and November 13th 1965. The number 18 is prominent with number 13 also appearing. Fátima is number 13. Garabandal is number 18. November 13th 1965 is establishing the connection between Garabandal and

Fátima. Apparitions in the months of June, July, August, October and November closely relate to Fátima and point again to end time events unfolding at the end of a certain year in the future.

During the apparitions at Garabandal, Mari Loli Mazon was told of a coming warning for the world and given the date of that warning which she chose to withhold.[4] Conchita Gonzalez was also given information relating to the warning. The warning is a celestial event that must begin with the letter A.

Pedro Regis of Anguera, Brazil was given information pertaining to the warning from Our Lady of Peace stating that it would occur on a Friday.

Message 3279, February 13th 2010

> "Dear sons and daughters, trust in the Lord. He will dry your tears and you will see a transformation in the world. Rejoice, for your names are already written in heaven. The calvary of humanity will begin on a Friday, but the victory of God will come afterwards and you will be led to a great day of victory. Human eyes have never seen what God has kept for

His chosen ones. Courage. Don´t get away from prayer. All this must happen (the actual events) but in the end will come the final triumph of My Immaculate Heart. I encourage you to tell everyone about My appeals. I need you very much. Stay firmly on the path I have pointed out. Trust fully in My motherly protection. I won´t abandon you. Forward without fear. This is the message I give you today in the name of the Most Holy Trinity. Thank you for permitting Me to reunite you here once more. I bless you in the name of the Father, and of the Son, and of the Holy Spirit. Amen. Be at peace."5

At Garabandal, Conchita Gonzalez was told of a coming miracle for the world which must occur within one year of the warning.6 She was given the date and time of this miracle but told not to disclose it until eight days before it is to occur. It has been confirmed that the miracle must be in the month of April. It must also fall on a Thursday at 8:30p.m. and between 7th and 17th of the month, but not on either of those days. The miracle must also fall on the feast day of a martyred saint of the Eucharist.

Conchita was told by Our Lady of Garabandal that the end was likely to follow closely after the miracle.

The Weeping Statue at Akita

Agnes Sasagawa had visitations from Our Lady of Akita on June 12th, July 6th, August 3rd and October 13th 1973.[7] The months that these apparitions appeared on, along with the final apparition on October 13th, were drawing a clear correlation with the miracles of Fátima.

The statue that wept had a total of 101 lacrimations from July 6th 1973 to September 15th 1981. Each lacrimation represents one year giving a total of 101 years. The lacrimations took place on nine separate years. Jacinta Marto died in the year 1920. Akita is indicating that the end time events described at Fátima would begin 110 years after Jacinta Marto's death in the year 2030.

The Miraculous Photo at Bayside

Veronica Lueken had her first apparition of Our Lady of the Roses at Saint Robert Bellarmine Church in Bayside, New York on June 18th 1970.[8] This established a direct connection with Garabandal. Her visions which took place from 1968 to 1995 focused primarily on end time events which very closely related those of Fátima.[9] The spread of communism across the world preceding the end of time was a common theme in Bayside and Fátima prophecies.

The ball of redemption mentioned in many of Veronica's visions is the sun's binary twin which is a brown dwarf shrouded in a huge iron oxide dust cloud. Interaction between the sun and its binary is the cause of the eleven-year solar cycle. The binary is both the redeemer and executioner at the end of time fulfilling God's work. This celestial body was also observed in the Sarah Menet prophecy.[10]

The Jacinta 1972 photo was given to Robert Franzenburg on September 14th 1971. He felt an electric charge pass through his hand when taking a photo outside St. Robert Bellarmine Church at Bayside, New York. The name Jacinta in the photo was that of Jacinta Marto establishing a connection between the Jacinta 1972 photo taken at Bayside and Fátima.

There are five parts to the Jacinta 1972 photo with parts one and two having been solved with part one providing confirmation of the Fátima third secret, the dark forces having entered high levels of the church by 1972, and the second part revealing the numbers 0, 2, and 3, and the letter P within the name Jacinta.[11] I will be providing the solutions to the three remaining parts: the Garabandal warning date and time, the Garabandal miracle date and time, and the date and time of the end of the world.

Decoding the Final Three Parts
of the Photo

Figure 1 – *Original Photo*

The reference point used to begin decoding the Jacinta 1972 photo was the year 2030 established at Akita. Akita indicated the year of the end which would also likely include the Garabandal miracle with the

Garabandal warning preceding the miracle by just less than one year.

Figure 2 – The 2 is Connected to the 0, 2 and 3

The 2 on its side and the 3 on its side in Figure 2 are suggesting that the digits following must come from the digits below. The thick line extending right from the end of the 2 at the end of 1972 is emphasising that a digit must follow the 2. The thick line extending right from the end of Jacinta is curving downwards suggesting a connection with the thick line extending right from the bottom of the digit 2 at the end of 1972. The thick line extending right from the bottom of the 2 at the end of 1972 is connecting to the thick line extending right from the end of Jacinta connecting the thick solid digit 2 at the end of 1972 to the solid digit 0 at the end of Jacinta. There is a line at the bottom left of the 0 connecting it to the 2 on its side. There is a horizontal line at the top of the 0 which extends right to left to the bottom of the 2 on its side. There is a vertical line which extends from the line connecting the 0 to the 2 on its side to the top of the t in Jacinta. This vertical line and the horizontal line intersect to form a cross. The top of the 0 connects to the horizontal line in the cross and this cross or plus connects the 0 to the 3 on its side.

The thick solid 2 at the end of 1972 must always be the first digit of any given year in the photo. The solid 0 at the end of Jacinta must always be the second digit of any given year in the photo. The dates and times of each event must be sequential with the month beginning with a capital letter followed by the day of month, followed by the year and finishing with the time. The time must be in the 24-hour format. In the following images, the month and day will be highlighted in red, the year in black and the time in yellow.

The Garabandal Warning Date and Time

Given that the Garabandal miracle is likely to occur between 7th and 17th of April 2030 and that the warning must occur within one year of the miracle, the warning must occur no earlier than the end of the first week of April 2029 and no later than mid-April 2030. It must be a celestial event beginning with the letter A, occur on a Friday and relate to an asteroid. It has to be Apophis which is due for a close fly by on Friday April 13th 2029. This is the 13 relating to Fátima. Apophis will be at its closest approach over the Atlantic just before 6 p.m. Eastern Daylight Time.

Figure 3 – *Day of Month and Year of Warning*

The l at the end of April in Figure 3 is an upside down thin vertical line leading into a thick line at the top of the 7 in 1972. The thick line at the end of l in April, moving right to left, is connecting to the thick line at the top of the digit 1 at the beginning of 1972. The first digit to follow April must be 1. The 1 at the beginning of 1972 is a thin vertical line with a thick line extending left from the top as observed in Figure 1. This connection with the l at the end of April, which is also a thin vertical line with thick line at the top, establishes this month as the month of the first date in the photo.

The thick line extending from the top of the digit 1 emphasises that another digit must follow the digit 1 and must begin with a thick line. The line running left from the J at the beginning of Jacinta extends downwards suggesting a connection with the line extending from the top of the 1 at the beginning of 1972. Connecting the line at the top of the 1 at the beginning of 1972 with the line extending downwards from the J and moving left to right leads to the bottom of the 3 on its side in Jacinta which begins with a thick line. The 3 must follow the 1 giving the month and day of the warning as April 13th.

Moving to the right of the 3 is the 2 on its side. When looking at the 2 from the original photo in Figure 1 and moving right to left, the digit 2 starts with a thin line, followed by a thick line, followed by a thin line, followed by a thick line, and finishes with a thin line next to the 3. The 9 in 1972 starts with a thin line on the right, followed by a thick line, at the top of the 9, followed by a thin line, followed by a thick line, and finishes with a thin vertical line. This establishes the connection between the 2 and 9. In Figure 3, the digit 9 must follow the 2. Starting with the 2 at the end of 1972, moving right connecting to the 0 at the end of Jacinta and 2 on its side and finishing with the 9 in 1972 establishes the year of the warning as 2029.

Figure 4 – *Impact Time of Apophis*

The impact time must follow sequentially from the end of the year 2029. In Figure 4, the digit 9 appears to have a dot on the top right. The impact time must be a four-digit sequence and cannot begin with a 9. The digit marked with a dot in the 9 must be the 1 which is flipped or inverted. The 7 following the 9 to the right also has a dot at the beginning of the digit on the right. There is also a dot at the bottom right of the digit 7. The 2 following the 7 is also marked with a dot on the right at the beginning of the digit. At the end of Jacinta, there is a dot at the end of the line extending right to the edge of the photo. The impact time must contain four digits. This dot implies that the fourth digit can be found within the name Jacinta on the top level.

Veronica Lueken had a vision on April 21st 1973 containing the following:

> Veronica: [sees writing in the sky, and spells out the letters]
>
> J – A – C – I – N – T – A. Now they're fading out, and there are numbers: 1-9-7-2 – 1-9-7-3. Now there's a large question mark, like this, next to the 3.
>
> Now that's fading out, like smoke being blown away. It was JACINTA 1972 – 1973,and then a large question mark. It's as though everything has exploded in the sky – the flash! And it's very hot! It's very warm! Oh! Oh! It feels like burning. Oh! Now the sky is very white. Colours – blues, purples – it's like a huge explosion. Now this voice, the voice… And the voice, Our Lady says, is a voice within you: your warning before chastisement! Flash, fire, and the voice within you. The final warning before chastisement![12]

The changing of the numbers in this vision from 1972 to 1973 followed by a question mark was confirming that the number 3 was the missing digit from the sequence and that is what must follow the number 7 in the impact time of the warning. In Figure 1, the number 3 on its side in Jacinta when approached from the left end is marked with a dot at the top and starts with a thick line, followed by a thin line, followed by a thick line, and finishes with a thin line next to the 2 on its side. The 7 in 1972 moving left to right starts with a thick line, followed by a thin line, followed by a thick line, at the top of the digit, and finishes with a thin vertical line. This establishes the connection between the 7 and the 3. In Figure 4, the inverted 1 taken from the 9 in 1972 is the first digit in the four-digit sequence. The 7 must be the second digit in the sequence and is followed by a dot which is then followed by the 3, finishing with the 2 at the end of 1972. This confirms the impact time of Apophis as 17:32 Eastern Daylight Time. The Garabandal warning date and time is Friday April 13th 2029 17:32 EDT.

Figure 5 – *Apophis Moving East West Impacting the Ocean*

A graphical representation of Apophis is contained within the Jacinta 1972 photo as illustrated in Figure 5. The asteroid is heading east west impacting the ocean with huge water displacement on each side. The shock wave flips or inverts the digit 1 taken from the 9 in 1972 which is the first digit in the four-digit sequence of the impact time of Apophis. This inversion symbolises the transformation of consciousness at the Garabandal warning in preparation for the miracle which is to follow.

Figure 6 – *Apophis in Jacinta 1972 Photo*

It is clearly shown in Figure 6 that the Jacinta 1972 photo contains the name Apophis.

The Garabandal Miracle Date and Time

The miracle must occur on a Thursday at 8:30 p.m. between 7th and 17th of the month and within one year of the warning. As the warning has been established as April 13th 2029, the miracle can only fall on one date and that is April 11th 2030.

Figure 7 – *Day of Month and Year of the Miracle*

In Figure 7, the l at the end of April is a solid thick line establishing a connection with the solid thick 2 at the end of 1972. This connection determines this month as being the month of the second date in the photo. The 1 at the end of April leads into the digit 1 at the beginning of 1972. This digit 1 is a short thick line at the top, followed by a thin vertical line. The 1 taken from the 9 in 1972 is inverted. This digit 1 begins just inside the starting point of the 9. The 9 begins on the right with a thin line. The inverted digit 1 is a short thick line at the top, followed by a thin vertical line. This establishes the connection between the inverted 1 and the 1 at the beginning of 1972. The digit 1 taken from the 9 must follow the digit 1 at the end of the 1 in April revealing the day and month of the miracle as April 11th. The second digit of the day of the month of the miracle, which is a flipped or inverted 1, symbolises the reversal of the miracle. The miracle is the reversal of present thought or full acceptance of the Holy Spirit which is the source of all healing.

In Figure 1, the 3 on its side in Jacinta, moving right to left, starts with a thin line, followed by a thick line, followed by a thin line, and finishes with a thick line. The 0 taken from the 9 in 1972 begins at the top of the thin vertical line in the 9. The 0 starts with a thin line, followed by a thick line, at the bottom of the 0, followed by a thin line, and finishes with a thick line, at the top of the 0, which ends at the thin vertical line in the 9. This establishes the connection between the 3 and 0 from the 9. In Figure 7, the 0 from the 9 must follow the 3, giving part of the year of the miracle. The 2 at the end of 1972 connects to the 0 at the end of Jacinta, which, moving left, connects to the 3 on its side which connects to the 0 from the 9 in 1972 giving the year of the miracle as 2030.

Figure 8 – *Time of Day of the Miracle*

The time of the miracle must flow sequentially from the year. In Figure 8, the last digit of the time is the 0 taken from the 9 in 1972 which is also the last digit in the year 2030 as established in Figure 7. The 0 taken from the 9 is connected to the 3 on its side in Jacinta. The 2 at the end of 1972 connects to the 0 at the end of Jacinta. There is a dot at the top right of the 0 which is also the right-hand side of the cross established in Figure 2. The cross connects the 0 to the 3 on its side which is followed by the 0 from the 9 directly below. This gives the miracle time of day as 20:30. The date and time of the Garabandal miracle is Thursday April 11th 2030 20:30 Central European Summer Time. Conchita Gonzalez of Garabandal stated that the miracle must coincide with the feast day of a martyred saint of the Eucharist. The miracle on April 11th 2030 coincides with the feast day of Stanislaus of Szczepanów who was a martyred saint of the Eucharist.

The Date and Time of the End of the World

The date of the end will likely follow closely after the miracle. Fátima is pointing to the end times beginning in October. Garabandal is indicating the end in December. Jesus told us to be ready to flee in the winter. The Sarah Menet prophecy is indicating that the world will begin to quake in winter. The date of the end of the world must come in December.

Figure 9 – *Day of Month and Year of End of the World*

There is a dot at the end of the r in December in Figure 9 which relates to the missing digit in the sequence giving the impact time of Apophis. This missing digit has been established in Figure 4 as the 3 on its side in Jacinta. The connection of the r at the end of December to the number 3 confirms December as the month of the third and final date in the photo.

The thick line at the end of the r in December is connecting to the thick line extending right from the 2 at the end of 1972. The first digit following December must be the 2. The thick line extending right from the bottom of the 2 at end of 1972 emphasises that another digit must follow the 2. This thick line leaves the edge of the photo and connects with the thick line extending from the top of the 1 at the beginning of 1972. The digit 1 must follow the 2 giving the day and month of the end as December 21st. Moving left to right, the 0 from the 9 in 1972 follows the 1 at the beginning of 1972. The 0 from the 9 is connected to the 3 on its side in Jacinta. The 2 at the end of 1972 connects to the 0 at the end of Jacinta, which, moving left, connects to the 3 on its side which connects to the 0 from the 9 revealing the year of the end of the world as 2030.

Figure 10 – *Time of Day of End of the World*

As the month and year of the end has been established as December 21st 2030, there had to be a connection to the Mayan end date and time of December 21st 2012 11:11. The date and time of the end must flow sequentially.

When the 0 has been taken from the 9 in 1972 in order to establish the year 2030, it leaves the inverted digit 1 in Figure 10. Moving to the left, the 1 taken from the 9 is connected to the digit 1 at the beginning of 1972 as established in Figure 7. There is a dot at the bottom right of the digit 1 at the beginning of 1972. Moving to the top of the digit 1 at the beginning of 1972 and moving left leads into another digit 1 on its side. The line extending left from the J at the beginning of Jacinta extends downwards forming a connection with the 1 on its side extending from the top of the 1 at the beginning of 1972. The line extending left from the J also forms another digit 1.

Starting from the inverted 1, taken from the 9 in 1972, and moving left to the 1 at the beginning of 1972 followed by a dot leading to the 1 on its side at the top of the digit 1 at the beginning of 1972 and followed by the final 1 on its side extending left from the J gives the time of day of the end of the world as 11:11. As this time relates to the entire world it must be Universal or Greenwich Mean Time. The date and time of the end of the world is December 21st 2030 11:11 Greenwich Mean Time. This is exactly eighteen years after the Mayan end date. This is the connection to the 18 of Garabandal. The first digit in the time of day of the end of the world is inverted symbolising the transformation of Heaven and Earth into a new Heaven and new Earth at the end of time. The month of June also appears in the Jacinta 1972 photo. June 2030 will mark the point in time when Earth changes begin to accelerate and all on Earth become aware that the end of time is approaching.

Figure 11 – *My Name is in the Photo*

In Figure 11, my name is shown in the Jacinta 1972 photo. This is not egotistical. It's necessary to demonstrate the miraculous nature of this photo. I was born on September 11th 1974. This photo was taken before I was born.

Confirmations and Conclusions

Tom Horn's Vision

Tom Horn received a vision from God in 2019 in which he saw two asteroids impact Earth.[13] One asteroid impacted the Pacific Ocean with the other impacting land. He was told at the end of the vision that the asteroid was Apophis and would impact on Friday April 13th 2029.

Pedro Regis of Anguera, Brazil received the following two messages from Our Lady of Peace both referring to Apophis.

May 21st 2005 Message 2525

"Something enormous will fall, and when it hits the water, it will cause great destruction. Regions on the earth will suffer, but whoever is with the Lord will receive comfort and peace."

Feb 14th 2005 Message 2641

"A giant mountain will travel the Pacific at high speed, causing great destruction in many regions. What I am saying should be taken seriously. Madagascar and Brazil will experience suffering."[14]

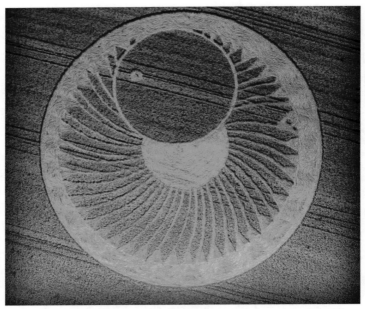

Figure 12 – Crop Circle at Cervia, Ravenna, Italy June 21st 2015[15]

Crop circles are pictorial messages given to humanity that will be understood by those with eyes to see. The Garabandal warning will be preceded by revolution in Rome. The crop circle in Figure 12 given to Cervia, Ravenna, Italy involving two asteroids is clearly referring to the Garabandal warning. The small circle represents Earth in its counter-clockwise orbital of the sun with the binary twin and its clockwise or retrograde sweeping arms approaching from behind the sun.

The Weeping Icon at the Russian Orthodox Church in Milan

A miracle took place at a Russian Orthodox church in 2010 in which an icon of Our Lady began to shed fragrant tears.[16] It began to weep on April 18th in 2010. A miracle relating to the month of April was the connection to the Garabandal miracle. It then began to weep again on April 18th in 2012. It began to weep a third time on April 17th in 2014. There was a three-year gap before it began to weep again on April 16th 2017. A pattern was beginning to emerge: a two-year gap between weeping's, followed by a two-year gap, followed by a three-year gap with enough information having been given, with the weeping's on these four separate years, to be able to confirm the date of the Garabandal miracle. Logically, the pattern would continue with another three-year gap before the next weeping began in April 2020. This is a Fibonacci spiral: a 2 by 2 square followed by a 3 by 3 square followed by a 5 by 5 square followed by an 8 by 8 square and so on as observed in Figure 13.

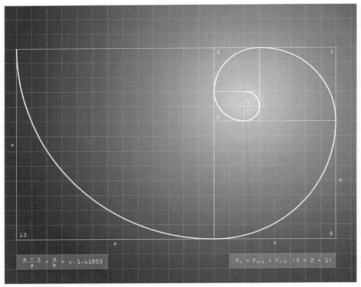

Figure 13 – *Fibonacci Spiral*[17]

The weeping of the icon began on April 18th in 2010 and was followed by weeping again on April 18th in 2012. In 2014, the weeping began on April 17th corresponding to a one-day drop at the beginning of the first three-year gap. This one-day drop relates to the transition from a 2 by 2 square to a 3 by 3 square in the Fibonacci spiral. In 2017, the weeping began on April 16th corresponding to another one-day drop at the beginning of the second three-year gap. Following this trend, the weeping would commence on April 14th in 2020 corresponding to a two-day drop at the beginning of the first five-year gap. This two-day drop relates to the transition from a 3 by 3 square to a 5 by 5 square in the Fibonacci spiral. The weeping would cease on the day of the miracle. The miracle cannot take place at the end of the first five-year gap as the weeping would cease on April 13th 2025 which is not a Thursday. Weeping would begin again on April 12th in 2025 corresponding to another two-day drop at the beginning of the second five-year gap.

If the weeping were to cease at the end of the second five-year gap that would confirm April 11th 2030 as the date of the miracle. If the weeping were to continue, the icon would weep again on April 9th 2030 corresponding to a three-day drop at the beginning of the first eight-year gap. This three-day drop relates to the transition from a 5 by 5 square to an 8 by 8 square in the Fibonacci spiral. The Garabandal miracle must occur between 7th and 17th of April but not on either of those two days. The weeping must cease at the end of the first eight-year gap on April 8th 2038. There is no martyred saint of the Eucharist celebrated on April 8th. The miracle must take place on April 11th 2030 on the feast day of Stanislaus of Szczepanów.

The weeping of this icon beginning on April 18th is reference to Garabandal, end of the world. The choosing of the Russian Orthodox Church at Milan relates to the warning and Russia invading Italy with the pope forced to flee Rome just prior to the Garabandal warning.

On Holy Thursday April 11th 1963 Conchita Gonzalez was told by Our Lady that a permanent sign would remain in the pines at Garabandal, following the miracle, that would endure until the end of time.[18] A luminous column would appear that could be seen and touched but not felt. The day and month that this information was given to Conchita is the day and month that the miracle will take place in the year 2030.

Crop Design in East Field, Alton Barnes, Wiltshire

Figure 14 *– Crop Design in East Field, Alton Barnes, Wiltshire August 2nd 2003*[19]

Each circle in Figure 14 is tilted at an angle of 23 degrees which represents Earth's polar magnetic axial lean or deviation from true north. The sweeping arms of the sun, which is Earth's host star, sweep Earth around in its orbital. The sweeping arms of the neutron star Sirius B, which is the sun's host star, sweep the sun around in its orbital. Earth periodically passes through varying concentrations of magnetic particles due to the effect the sweeping arms of Sirius B have on the sun. This results in Earth experiencing three magnetic trimesters per year.

The summer trimester from May to August is most active. In the trimester from September to December the particle flow is diminishing. The trimester from January to April is a quiescent period leading into the active summer trimester. Each circle in Figure 13 represents one magnetic trimester. The crop square in the formation of a spiral is the connection to the Fibonacci spiral. The weeping icon at the Russian Orthodox Church in Milan provides the start date of April 18th 2010 for this countdown. This countdown of sixty-two trimesters of four months each, or twenty years and eight months, provides confirmation that the date of the end will be eight months after the Garabandal miracle and must take place in December 2030. The final six trimesters, or two-year period, marked in red will be a time of great upheaval for Earth which will include the beginning of glacial rebound as detailed in the Sarah Menet prophecy.

On Christmas Day in 2020, I was at home on my own getting ready to leave the house to have a meal at my mother's home. I have an old DECT cordless phone in my home that makes a very distinct noise when the phone is placed back onto the charging base. The phone was resting on the charger and just before leaving, I heard that distinct noise ring out as if someone had placed the phone back onto the charger. A few seconds later, it rang out again followed a few seconds later by the same noise and one final ringing a few seconds later. It seemed like an anomaly at the time and it wasn't until April of 2021 that I came to realise that those four ring tones were signalling December 21st. It was a series of miracles drawing my attention to the day and month of the end of the world.

Saint Tarcisius

Conchita Gonzalez stated during one of her visions at Garabandal that the miracle would fall on the date of a martyred saint of the Eucharist related to the following description:

> "After mass, he took consecrated hosts to imprisoned Christians awaiting martyrdom. As a boy, he would be less suspect making the visit than were he a man. As he travelled to the prison along the Roman road known as

the Appian Way, he ran into a group of pagan boys and men who began to harass him. While they did not know, specifically, he belonged to the hidden group of Christians, they demanded he show them what he had in his hands, which were hiding in his clothes. Tarcisius refused, knowing they would likely take and desecrate the Blessed Sacrament if they got it from him. His continued refusal angered the crowd who began to assault him. As the angry mob beat him, Tarcisius fell to the stones of the Appian Way shielding the host beneath his body. The mob did not relent once he fell and eventually killed him. When they rolled his body over to discover what he had been hiding, they found nothing. The host had vanished."[20]

The feast day of Tarcisius is August 15th. The miracle must fall between 7th and 17th of April. Pope Damasus ordered the above text to be inscribed upon the tomb of Tarcisius. The connection between Tarcisius and the miracle of Garabandal is Pope Damasus whose feast days fall on 11th December in the Catholic Church and November 13th in the Orthodox Church. The number 11 is the day of the miracle and 13 is the day of the warning. November is the beginning of serious Earth changes in the apocalypse and December is the date of the end of the world.

Final Thoughts

Astrophysicists have determined that Apophis will not impact Earth at its next closest approach on April 13th 2029. When Apophis does impact Earth on that day, they will be at a loss to explain how its orbital was altered setting it on a collision course with Earth. What may appear as just a natural occurrence to some on that day will appear as the supernatural to many others.

The Garabandal miracle will be an event which will open a temporary window into heaven. Heavenly figures will appear amidst a rainbow of colours. The presence of God will be felt in the heart with all present having a direct encounter with Christ who is the source of all healing. Conchita Gonzalez will announce the miracle eight days in advance with the date and time coinciding exactly with the date and time revealed in the Jacinta 1972 photo. "For God speaketh once, yea twice," the book of Job 33:14. The aligning of these dates and times will lead to confirmation and acceptance of the date and time of the end of the world in the Jacinta 1972 photo.

The events of the apocalypse will be both frightening and beautiful at the same time. The end of time is about acceptance not rejection. It is about who we are not what we have. Those who come to understand the all-powerful and incorruptible nature of the presence of God will see this illusory material world fade away. A huge destruction in the eyes of some will be a creation in the eyes of others. Jacinta 1972 in bright writing beneath the blue tree leaves in the Jacinta 1972 photo symbolises graduation day. We are the holy children awaiting graduation. Persevere until the end. The end of time is a date with destiny, it is our time. It is time to get right with God.

Bibliography

Alexander Steve. Copyright Holder. 2022.Use of image acquired. Last accessed: March 13 2022.https:// temporarytemples.co.uk/

Association Our Lady of Anguera. 2021. Last accessed: March 1 2022.https://www.apelosurgentes.com.br/en-us/ mensagens/ano/2010/

Catholic Saint Medals. 2022. Last accessed: March 13 2022. https://catholicsaintmedals.com/saints/st-tarcisius/

The Coming Great Events Upon Mankind. These Last Days Ministries, Inc(1996–2018). Last accessed: March 1 2022. https://baysidemessages.tistory.com/m/451

De Marchi, John. The True Story of Fatima. Last accessed: February 26 2022.https://fatima.org/wp-content/ uploads/2017/03/The-True-Story-of-Fatima.pdf

The Encyclopaedia of Religious Phenomena."Our Lady of the Roses Mary Help of Mothers"2018. Last accessed: March

1 2022.https://encyclopedia2.thefreedictionary.com/ Our+Lady+of+the+Roses%2C+Mary+Help+of+Mothers

Isaiah 24:20. Bible Hub (2004–2012).Last Accessed: February 26 2022.https://biblehub.com/isaiah/24-20.htm

Jamie, Fibonacci Sequence – Golden Spiral, Adobe Stock. Last accessed: March 13 2022.https://stock.adobe.com/ uk/images/fibonacci-sequence-golden-spiral/50215601 Extended licence acquired.

LaViolette, Paul. The Date Revealed at Garabandal for the Coming World Miracle. The Sphinx Stargate. 2013. Last accessed: March 13 2022.https://etheric.com/the-date-revealed-at-garabandal-for-the-coming-world-miracle/

Menet, Sarah Lanelle. There Is No Death: The Extraordinary True Experience of Sarah Lanelle Menet. Mountain Top Publishing, 1 December 2002.

The Miracle. Interview With Conchita. 1973. 1260.org (2012–2021). Last accessed March 1 2022.http://www.1260.org/ Mary/Apparitions_Garabandal/Garabandal_Apparitions_ Miracle_Conchita_en.htm

Mother of God. GARABANDAL LIBRARY. GARABANDAL INFO & ANSWERS. April 11 2021. Last accessed: May 17 2022. https://motheofgod.com/ threads/garabandal-info-answers.11105/page-193

Our Lady of Akita 1973–1975. Servants of the Pierced Hearts of Jesus and Mary. 2013.Last accessed: February 27 2022. https://piercedhearts.org/hearts_jesus_mary/apparitions/akita.html

Our Lady of the Roses Mary Help of Mothers. Last accessed: March 1 2022.http://www.ourladyoftheroses.org/ourladyoftheroses/images/The_Messages/VigilMessages/Jacinta%201972%20-%20Booklet.pdf

Schucman, Helen. A Course in Miracles: Combined Volume. Foundation for Inner Peace; 3rd edition, 21 May 2008.

The Story of Garabandal. Home of the Mother Foundation. 2019. Last accessed: February 28 2022.https://garabandal.it/en/about/a-brief-history/story-of-garabandal

Tom Horn Dies and God Shows Him the Future, Supernatural Stories(2020). Google LLC. Last accessed: March 1 2022. https://www.youtube.com/watch?v=_cWH2UPLQgU

The Warning and Miracle. Interviews With the Seers. St. Michael's Garabandal Center for Our Lady of Carmel Inc. Taken from Garabandal International Magazine (October–December2004). Last accessed: February 28 2022. http://www.garabandal.org/News/Garabandal_Warning_Miracle_Interviews.shtml

Endnotes

1   Isaiah 24:20. Bible Hub (2004-2012). Last Accessed: February 26 2022. https://biblehub.com/isaiah/24-20.htm

2   John de Marchi, I.M.C. The True Story of Fatima. Last accessed: February 26 2022. https://fatima.org/wp-content/uploads/2017/03/The-True-Story-of-Fatima.pdf

3   The Story of Garabandal. Home of the Mother Foundation. 2019.Last accessed: February 28 2022.https://garabandal.it/en/about/a-brief-history/story-of-garabandal

4   The Warning and Miracle. Interviews With the Seers. St. Michael's Garabandal Center for Our Lady of Carmel Inc. Taken from Garabandal International Magazine (October–December2004). Last accessed: February 28 2022. http://www.garabandal.org/News/Garabandal_Warning_Miracle_Interviews.shtml

5   Association Our Lady of Anguera. 2021.Last accessed: March 1 2022. https://www.apelosurgentes.com.br/en-us/mensagens/ano/2010/

6   The Miracle. Interview With Conchita. 1973. 1260.org (2012-2021). Last accessed: March 1 2022.http://www.1260.org/Mary/Apparitions_Garabandal/Garabandal_Apparitions_Miracle_Conchita_en.htm

7   Our Lady of Akita 1973–1975. Servants of the Pierced Hearts of Jesus and Mary. 2013. Last accessed: February 27 2022.https://piercedhearts.org/hearts_jesus_mary/apparitions/akita.html

8   The Encyclopaedia of Religious Phenomena."Our Lady of the Roses Mary Help of Mothers".2018. Last accessed: March 1 2022.https://encyclopedia2.thefreedictionary.com/Our+Lady+of+the+Roses%2C+Mary+Help+of+Mothers

9   The Coming Great Events Upon Mankind. These Last Days Ministries, Inc(1996–2018). Last accessed: March 1 2022.https://baysidemessages.tistory.com/m/451

10   Sarah Lanelle Menet. There Is No Death: The Extraordinary True
     Experience of Sarah Lanelle Menet, Mountain Top Publishing, 1
     December 2002.

11   Our Lady of the Roses Mary Help of Mothers. Last accessed: March
     1 2022.http://www.ourladyoftheroses.org/ourladyoftheroses/images/
     The_Messages/VigilMessages/Jacinta%201972%20-%20Booklet.pdf

12   Our Lady of the Roses Mary Help of Mothers(Page 3). Last accessed:
     March 1 2022.http://www.ourladyoftheroses.org/ourladyoftheroses/
     images/The_Messages/VigilMessages/Jacinta%201972%20-%20
     Booklet.pdf

13   Tom Horn Dies and God Shows Him the Future, Supernatural Stories
     (2020). Google LLC. Last accessed: March 1 2022.https://www.
     youtube.com/watch?v=_cWH2UPLQgU

14   Association Our Lady of Anguera.2021. Last accessed: March 1 2022.
     https://www.apelosurgentes.com.br/en-us/mensagens/ano/2010/

15   Lorenzo Franciosi. Copyright Holder. Permission to use image granted.

16   Paul LaViolette. The Date Revealed at Garabandal for the Coming
     World Miracle. The Sphinx Stargate. 2013. Last accessed: March 13
     2022.https://etheric.com/the-date-revealed-at-garabandal-for-the-
     coming-world-miracle/

17   Jamie, Fibonacci Sequence – Golden Spiral, Adobe Stock. Last accessed:
     March 13 2022.https://stock.adobe.com/uk/images/fibonacci-
     sequence-golden-spiral/50215601 Extended licence acquired.

18   Mother of God. GARABANDAL LIBRARY. GARABANDAL INFO
     & ANSWERS. April 11 2021. Last accessed: May 17 2022. https://
     motheofgod.com/threads/garabandal-info-answers.11105/page-193

19   Steve Alexander. Copyright Holder.2022. Use of image acquired. Last
     accessed: March 13 2022.https://temporarytemples.co.uk/

20   Catholic Saint Medals. 2022. Last accessed: March 13 2022.https://
     catholicsaintmedals.com/saints/st-tarcisius/

Made in United States
North Haven, CT
01 February 2023

31984154R00035